What Kind of Animal Is It?

Monkeys and Other Primates

Rebecca Sjonger and Bobbie Kalman

A Crabtree Crown Book

Crabtree Publishing
crabtreebooks.com

Monkeys and Other Primates

Editor-in-chief
Bobbie Kalman

Writing team
Rebecca Sjonger
Bobbie Kalman

Substantive editor
Kelley MacAulay

Editors
Molly Aloian
Robin Johnson
Kathryn Smithyman

Design
Margaret Salter

Consultant
Patricia Loesche, Ph.D., Animal Behavior Program, Department of Psychology, University of Washington

Production manager
Candice Campbell

Images
Barbara Bedell: page 7 (gorilla);
All other images: Shutterstock.com

Crabtree Publishing

crabtreebooks.com 800-387-7650

In Canada: We acknowledge the financial support of the Government of Canada through the Canada Book Fund for our publishing activities.

Printed in the U.S.A./CP032026

Published in Canada
Crabtree Publishing
616 Welland Ave.
St. Catharines,
Ontario L2M 5V6

Published in the United States
Crabtree Publishing
347 Fifth Ave.
Suite 1402-145
New York, NY 10016

Hardcover: 978-1-0398-7321-6
Paperback: 978-1-0398-7379-7
Ebook (pdf): 978-1-0398-7428-2
Epub: 978-1-0398-7477-0

Library and Archives Canada Cataloguing in Publication
Available at Library and Archives Canada

Library of Congress Cataloging-in-Publication Data
Available at the Library of Congress

Contents

All kinds of primates!

Primates are animals. There are many **species**, or kinds of primates. Each primate belongs to a group. There are four groups of primates. The four groups are shown on these pages.

1. The largest group of primates is called Old World monkeys.

tamarin

marmoset

New World monkey

2. Another group of primates is called New World monkeys. Marmosets, tamarins, and New World monkeys make up this group.

gibbon

chimpanzee

gorilla

orangutan

bonobo

3. Apes and humans make up another group of primates. There are many species of apes. Apes include gibbons, gorillas, bonobos, orangutans, and chimpanzees. There is only one human species.

lemur

bushbaby

loris

4. Lorises, tarsiers, bushbabies, and lemurs belong to a group of primates called prosimians.

tarsier

Primates are mammals

Primates are **mammals**. All mammals have **backbones** inside their bodies. A backbone is a group of bones in the middle of an animal's back.

These Old World monkeys have backbones.

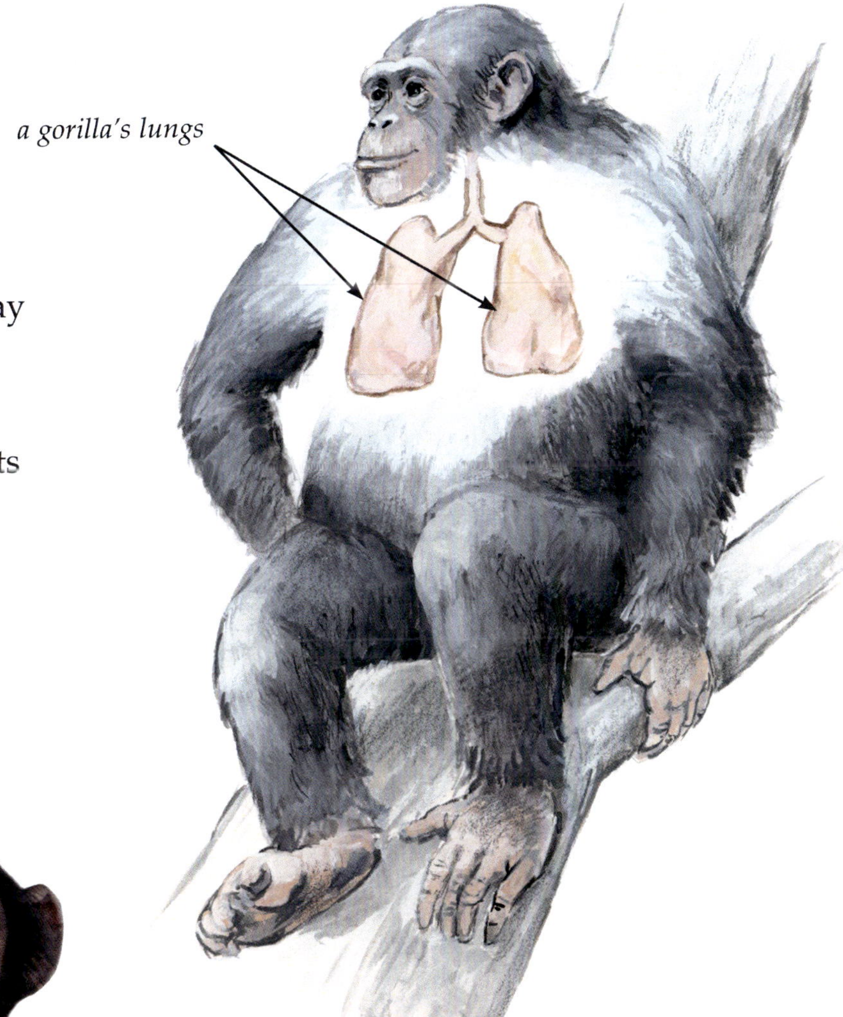

Breathing air

Mammals breathe air to stay alive. Like all mammals, primates breathe air using **lungs**. Lungs are body parts that take in air. Lungs also let out air.

More about mammals

Mammals are animals that

- **nurse** when they are babies (See page 21.)
- are **warm-blooded** (See page 8.)
- have fur or hair on their bodies (See page 9.)

Warm blood

Like all mammals, primates are **warm-blooded** animals. The bodies of warm-blooded animals always stay about the same temperature, in both hot weather and cold weather.

These snow monkeys live in Japan. Japan is warm in summer, but cold in winter. A snow monkey's body temperature is the same in summer as it is in winter.

Fur or hair

All primates have fur or hair on their bodies. Most primates have fur. Their fur helps keep them warm and dry.

People have hair on their bodies. The girl on the right has long hair.

Different primates have fur of different colors. These lemurs have black-and-white fur. Their fur is silky.

Primate bodies

All primates have arms, legs, hands, and feet. Primates also have fingers and toes. Most primates have thumbs. They use their fingers, toes, and thumbs to hold objects. All primates have nails on their fingers and toes. Having nails helps primates pick up small objects. Some primates have tails. A few primates can hold objects using their tails.

This orangutan grabs onto vines using its fingers and toes.

Big or small?

The bodies of different primates are different sizes. Some primates have large bodies. Gorillas are the largest primates. Other primates have small bodies. Mouse lemurs are some of the smallest primates.

A mouse lemur's body is about the same size as a mouse's body.

Male gorillas, such as the one shown above, are the largest primates.

Primate homes

Different primates live in different parts of the world. Most primates live in places where the weather is always warm. Other primates live in places that are warm in summer and cold in winter.

Many primates live in Africa and South America. These places are always warm. The baboons in this picture live in Africa. Baboons are Old World monkeys.

Primates with small bodies spend more time in trees than they do on the ground. This New World monkey lives mainly in trees.

In the trees

Most primates live in forest **habitats**. A habitat is the natural place where an animal lives. Many primates are good climbers! They spend a lot of time in trees. Primates climb trees using their strong arms, hands, legs, and feet. Other primates use their strong legs to leap from tree to tree.

Primates with large bodies spend most of their time on the ground. Chimpanzees usually stay on the ground.

Food and water

Different primates eat different foods. Some primates are **herbivores**. Herbivores are animals that eat mainly plants. A few primates are **carnivores**. Carnivores are animals that eat other animals. Most primates are **omnivores**. Omnivores are animals that eat both plants and other animals.

Tarsiers are carnivores. They eat animals such as lizards, birds, and insects. This tarsier is eating an insect.

Large primates often look for food during the day. Chimpanzees are large primates. They look for food during the day. Small primates look for food at night.

Crowned lemurs are herbivores. They eat mainly fruit.

Thirsty primates

Primates need to drink water to stay alive. They often drink from puddles. They scoop up water using their hands. The monkey on the right is using its hands to scoop up water from a river. Some primates use leaves to collect water. They soak the leaves in water and then squeeze the water into their mouths.

Groups called troops

Most kinds of primates live in groups. These groups are called **troops**. Some primate troops are large. Large troops may have over 20 primates! Other primate troops are small. Small troops may have only two primates.

Large troops are made up of many males, females, and young primates. Mountain gorillas live in large troops.

Part of a family

A primate troop is like a family. The older primates in the troop take care of the younger primates. Young primates, such as this baby monkey, learn by watching older primates. They learn how to find food, collect water, and climb trees.

Sending messages

Primates send messages to one another in different ways. They often use sounds and actions to send messages. Some primates hoot or grunt to greet one another. Primates may also stomp their feet or hold out their hands when they are begging for food.

This Old World monkey is showing its sharp teeth. It seems to be angry or excited. Monkeys also roar loudly to warn other animals to stay away!

Chimpanzees often kiss and hug each other to make up after a fight!

Musical messages

Gibbons send messages by making loud high-pitched calls. These calls are known as **songs**. Gibbons may sing songs to warn other animals to stay away. Some gibbons sing for as long as fifteen minutes without stopping!

This gibbon is singing to keep other animals away.

Primate babies

Primate babies are born. Animals that are born are not inside eggs when they come out of the bodies of their mothers. Both mother and father primates care for their babies. Other members of the troop may also watch over the babies.

Most primate mothers give birth to one or two babies at a time.

Drinking milk

Primate parents care for their babies for at least one year. The babies drink milk from the bodies of their mothers. Drinking mother's milk is called nursing. The babies nurse many times a day. As they get older, the young primates stop nursing. They find their own food.

This baby primate is nursing.

Many monkeys!

There are more than 80 kinds of Old World monkeys! Old World monkeys live in Africa, Asia, and Europe. Most species of Old World monkeys live mainly in trees. Many have short tails. They cannot hold objects with their tails. Old World monkeys hold objects using their thumbs and their big toes.

Old World monkeys, such as this baboon, have pads of skin on their bottoms.

Primates with pouches

Many species of Old World monkeys have **pouches** inside their mouths. Pouches are small pockets. The monkeys fill their pouches with food. They carry the food back to their troops and share it with the other monkeys.

This Old World monkey is filling its pouches with grass and leaves.

A few species of Old World monkeys, such as macaques, live mainly on the ground. These macaques are eating grass and plants.

More monkey business

New World monkeys, marmosets, and tamarins live in Central America and South America. These primates live only in trees. They do not spend time on the ground. Most New World monkeys can hang from branches using their long tails. Most marmosets and tamarins cannot use their tails to hang from branches.

Marmosets and tamarins use their sharp claws to hold on to tree branches. The primates above are tamarins.

What is the difference?

New World monkeys do not look the same as Old World monkeys. The charts on this page show how these monkeys are different.

Old World monkeys

- Old World monkeys have nostrils that point downward.
- Old World monkeys can hold objects using their thumbs.
- Old World monkeys have pads on their bottoms.

New World monkeys

- New World monkeys have nostrils that point sideways.
- New World monkeys cannot hold objects using their thumbs.
- New World monkeys do not have pads on their bottoms.

All about apes

Bonobos, chimpanzees, gorillas, orangutans, and gibbons are all known as apes. Apes live mainly in Africa and Asia. You can tell if a primate is an ape by looking at its bottom! Unlike many other primates, apes do not have tails.

Many apes build nests using tree branches and leaves.

Harmless herbivores

Apes are the strongest primates. Most apes are herbivores. They eat a lot of food, such as fruits, leaves, and flowers. The mountain gorilla shown right is eating leaves.

Most apes spend time in trees and on the ground. Gibbons spend most of their time in trees. Their bodies are smaller than the bodies of most other apes. Gibbons are good climbers and swingers. They swing from branch to branch faster than other apes can.

Prosimians

This loris uses its large eyes to look for insects at night.

Prosimians live in Africa and Asia. They live mainly in trees. Most prosimians look for food at night. They have large eyes that help them see in the dark. Lorises, such as the one on the left, move slowly through the trees. They eat caterpillars and other insects that move slowly, too.

Ring-tailed lemurs are among the few prosimians that spend time on the ground. Other prosimians stay high up in trees. These ring-tailed lemurs are resting on a fallen tree.

Where in the world?

Primates live in many parts of the world. Most primates live in South America, Africa, and Asia. Some primates live in Europe and Central America. Look at the map below and then answer the questions on page 31.

1. Old World monkeys live on three continents. Turn to page 22 to find out where they live.

2. This bushbaby is a prosimian. On which continents do prosimians live? Turn to page 28 for a clue.

3. This chimpanzee is part of the ape group. Where does it live? Think hard! Turn to page 26 for help.

4. Primates in the New World monkey group live in two parts of the world. See page 24 to find out where they live.

Answers

1. Africa, Asia, and Europe
2. Africa and Asia
3. Africa and Asia
4. South America and Central America

Words to know and Index

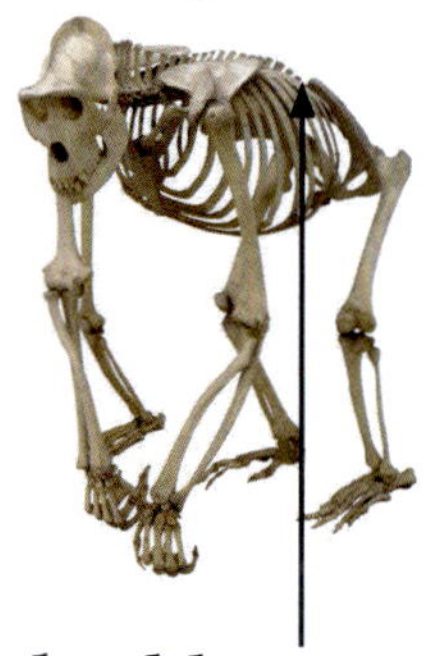

Other index words